THE HOUSE
OF THE
EASILY AMUSED

Also by Shelley A. Leedahl:

THE HOUSE
OF THE EASILY AMUSED

Shelley A. Leedahl

For Colleen + Kevin —

Wishing you all good things.

Shelley Leedahl

2011

OOLICHAN BOOKS
LANTZVILLE, BRITISH COLUMBIA, CANADA
2008

Library and Archives Canada Cataloguing in Publication

Leedahl, Shelley A. (Shelley Ann), 1963-

The house of the easily amused / Shelley A. Leedahl.

Poems. ISBN 978-0-88982-239-9

I. Title.

PS8573.E3536H68 2008   C811'.54   C2007-907668-8

We gratefully acknowledge the financial support of the Canada
Council for the Arts, the British Columbia Arts Council through
the BC Ministry of Tourism, Small Business and Culture, and the
Government of Canada through the Book Publishing Industry
Development Program, for our publishing activities.

Cover photo by Shelley A. Leedahl

Published by   .
Oolichan Books
P.O. Box 10, Lantzville
British Columbia, Canada
V0R 2H0

Printed in Canada

For my family, broadly defined

CONTENTS

Mérida, and after

Snow so barely there: Banff poems

Hands like my mother's: Saskatchewan, and elsewhere

Europa, Europa

"Don't be careful."

—Juan José Rodríguez
Mérida, Mexico

MÉRIDA, AND AFTER

⌁ Upon not once phoning home ⌁

I'd been living in simple dresses
where leaves shuttered sky, talking to small animals,
measuring my mornings in animals: two raccoons
and a rabbit.
                        (Also eight pelicans.)

I'd grown too fond of windows
and watching rain arrive from the north.

Mérida.

A million people and ways
to get the language, weather, dance steps wrong.

Serpentine streets and a mountain of bags
in a low-down cab, the hotel address
a damp scrap harboured inside my head
like one more childhood prayer.

Isadore's hurricane signature in masticated trees. Sidewalks
stooked with glass and tin: reflective altars.

At Hotel San Juan, pink hibiscus
the size of fists
break hearts beyond my door. I trace leaves
in the mirror frame, mark the ceiling fan's rhythm.

Dos mapaches y un conejo.

También ocho pelicanos.

All the things I know will be of no use here.

❧ Downpour ❧

I stand in the bathroom curling my eyelashes;
smooth jazz syncopates the evening

with its eloquent colleague, rain. On the dressing table
a loaf of sweet bread half eaten, poorly wrapped

among rotting tangerines. It's all ahead
of us: night along the corridor, minor movements

in each hotel room. We open doors, unshutter
windows. An invitation to *las brisas,* to whomever

should pass. How little it takes. On the avenue
a woman plaits rain through her hair; below her

the undulation of stones. Last night in Umán, bats
big as pigeons ballet'd between trees

and the convent. Everything and the moon
swooned. I paused on the curb, swimsuit damp

beneath my dress, felt lungs collapse
like red balloons let go. How will we manage

not to stumble toward love, he with her,
those three? Upstairs and down: desire and notes,

surreptitious. To live in a room lit only by lightning,
hummingbirds drunk on hibiscus. Soon streets

will be rivers and we shall dance. Thunder is heavy beds
dragged across slate. Mérida must be sipped.

⁀ Sisal
(for those who were there) ⁀

The moon's hand in it. Habitual knotting of moments
in a rented car compelled toward land's end. Sky exhaling
stars. Pier, white pails, fishermen. What continues

to swim. A fortune of bones left on plates, downed bottles
of *Negra Modelo.* Beside the parked car a rodeo
of thin dogs deliberate in shadows and five figures

scrape salt from limbs, lean *paso a paso* toward another
infinite instant. The sea, *las brisas,* bare feet finding
the cool hum of night beneath the weight of sand.

Sudden knowledge of light above and behind. O firefly.
O falling stars on our shoulders. Words phosphorescent
in the sand's wet skin, this constellation we've become,

blind explorations into the soundless dark, collective
breath held in one chest, blood of a single heart.
That pulse. Two weeks ago we were strangers. Now this,

so goddamn perfect it's unfair to the rest of the world.
Can't imagine a future, a day without these four living
somewhere inside it. Soon my return to the country

of extremes. Push it back, let it fade off the map
as we've grown to understand it. Night bleeds more
stars, fireflies. Moonscape. To leave now

or ever is unconscionable; this moment
I'll measure the rest of my life against.
The songs we sang. The songs we sang.

To Aké in a borrowed van

Abandoned house, weeds softening stone,
aphotic rectangle in the beckoning

shape of a door. Inside: the umbra
of a tomb, yet vines

Rapunzel down walls.

                              I release my bladder
in a back room, listening to birds.

I've lost my friends; not at the ruined factory
or beside the ravenous sheep.

Everywhere is green seeping into ruins, seeping into hills.

Corrugated steel-flash from treetops:
                         the hurricane's spelled its name.

A sudden vortex of citrine butterflies
lights off skin and hair.

Four thousand winged pansies.

(So little's a lifetime commitment, so long
since I was last conceived.)

To a bare-legged boy on a too-small bike:
 Estoy buscando a mis amigos.

We snake-trail the village,
                                    barely looking.

ᔃ Mercado ᔂ

All day I felt like falling.

I could not inhale the carnival
of eels, octopi, grey sharks. A bowl brimming

with fried gills. Aisles of elbows and voice crush.
Peppers, corn, candy, carnations.

A stall for repairing saints.

Machetes laid out beside dog collars.
Racks of *huaraches* and sunglasses.

Caged birds, rodents, the man who kept after us:

> *Whatever you want . . . boa constrictor, anything*
> *illegal . . . I get for you.*

Tortilla women. Gold merchants. Cinnamon heat.
Little boys dancing for coins.

The barefoot knife-sharpener
with explosive hair.

(Also the drunk passed out near the vegetables,
pants shamed with urine, skin alive
in flies.)

The kind of music
a man makes
with two plastic pop bottles

and a chorus of stones.

✑ You hardly knew me ✑

Now I understand why it hurts

to see myself
in the photo you shot
on the vacuous street.

        You captured me

as Alfred Stieglitz
caught his Georgia
in 1918.

      I am the shape of a woman
inclined against rock. A photograph

that says *Here I am,*
this is who I am,
              this is the way

you should remember me.

From the balcony of La Bella Epoca
(notes from an artists' exchange)

Raindrops smash on Mayan ground.
(Something to do with faith?)

Café-view of the one-toothed vagrant
in the concrete park, always chewing bread
and reading the same page of a book
between lovers benched
on the S-shaped *confidencialies*.

A man sells *hamacas*
within the crossfire of traffic. Window-doves:
    his hands.

On the gallery steps,
        a philosopher teases apple-skin
while a Mestizo saws a rag
across his boots.

So forever it goes on—

        torturing bites.
        The shoeshiner's raw knees.

Afternoon's turning to stone
                        and slow falling
of civilizations.
        (I rarely think of home.)

⤳ Laura dancing with a short man ⤳

How soon each scene becomes memory,
a worry that details will be lost

                              or rearranged
even as events are unfolding
and the band plays on.

This is certain:

I sat at a street-side table with friends and electricity
slalomed between us. A short man
asked Laura to dance.

                (She may have worn braids.)

Best dancer among us, she gave lessons
in Andrés' room. We up-ended the bed, shucked shoes.

An hour before, I was cooling in the pool.

———

                    You see how it happens.

This began with Laura, a short man,
their street dance. Pants constrictive, his belly
    preceded him.

The songs soon turned familiar;
by the end almost everyone danced.

                              Ernie on *la calle*
before his flight left:
        If my friends could see me now.

The pirate in the park with his single tooth.

Don, Lilian, Salvador, Ximena,
Maleea, Andrés, Gerardo, José and Juan José.

I deliver their names
as a litany. Speak them as a poem.

∾ The house of the easily amused
   (Chuburná revisited) ∾

Today is sweaterish.

Cappuccino sea-churn
and no point talking against ill-tempered wind. We scatter

like the seeds Andrés broadcast
on a blanket and read in a language
he alone comprehends.

(I ferry thimble-sized shells in the bell of my skirt.)

Miners of narratives from blue-tiled rooms; we ghost
through storm-ravaged beach houses.

Out and in—the tide of us—

                              until we settle

arms apart
on the weather-driven sand
erasing kicked-off thongs and huaraches.

(Another scene from the cinema-life.)

Sea salt between Maleea's dress straps;
Gerardo's candescent-white pants on leopard skin.
A low bench of driftwood; Juan José deep in Borges.
And Andrés, decoding the tubercular sea.

Back in the rented Nissan, a game lacking rules
or objective: *Fiction or poetry?*
          Two hands or one leg?
          Electroshock or electrocardiogram?

The Yucatán's other story: jungle serpents,
cenotes, apple-boxed bones.

I will turn old unwinding this.

⇒ Saying *buenas noches* ⇐

"We spend the first two weeks arriving, the last two
    trying not to leave."
                                —Maleea Acker, Mérida

Foot of the stairs by the message board, near a cooler
perpetually locked.

No one wants to be first.

The Canadians still too reserved to embrace
the Mexicans or each other, though I sense
the distance lessening, my own need
rising by degrees. (Maybe tomorrow
I'll lean into this
                    familia we are becoming.)

Can't fathom final countdown—

    Back to the prairies, I say.
    Back to the biggest city in the world, Gerardo says.

What would nights add up to
                        without the polyglottic stars?

We bother Fausto to unlock the cooler,
sell us more bottled water to line up in our rooms.

So easily I've assumed this other woman. I rarely know
the date, have forgotten the news of the world.

How in the air I am. How hovering.

And now the hour is late.

O bridges in cities whose architecture awaits us.
I've ventured outside the fence of my life, left

                              the blue gate swinging.

⬿ How the world looks from the observation deck at
   the Minneapolis-St. Paul International Airport ⬿

Cool and blue, moon
a one-dollar coin beneath clouds' embroidery,
jets in queue like a spoiled kid's toys. Final stop
this five-hour limbo
before she greets prairie
husband and daughter, who'll bring her coat
(and, she hopes, socks).

Weeks since they've spoken.

                    Up there it's fine.

Tarmac's black-shining, elevator jazz
easing transitions
between public addresses: lost items, gate changes,
and listen, again
                    they're calling her name.

☙ Afterthought ☙

Everything white: snow-veil, walls, the unwavering
interior silence broken only by the furnace
stammering in.

   Outside, wind-rattle: the Russian olive sunders.

Winter came quickly while I was away;
the trees had no time to undress.

Fifth day back and first return to the country,
my wit's-end shack by the woods.

         And finally I catch my breath.

Today I scarcely keep myself in paper, words
soaking pages like wine welts a tablecloth,
thoughts a chivvy of birds
                        brushing wingtips
as they're lured north and south.

The airport faces of friends
                           —farewells.

I imagine Andrés and Maleea in Havana, her long hair
escaping the green scarf's order,
humidity's tacky hand on her nape.

A sun-tiled garden
for Gerardo, slow-turning pages of a book
he will read again.

Perhaps Juan José, like me, is alone
and remembering
how he danced best of all in the sand.
        Near the end we sifted
through an inventory of prints: two photos
caught our Celestún salsa.

  I loved you that day: spherules
                        skipped across water.

In another room, radio tuned low,
                my good husband
sketches my photos.

⮜ Mariposas ⮞

The grace of afternoon sleep, day's penultimate light.
A map of three countries perpetually spread.

Given a choice, this is the hour of winter
I'll one day depart from. Village streets quiescent, sky
between evergreens reserved and pink
as the ear's private paths.

At dusk yesterday I arrived to a storybook town,
Christmas lights framed every house: gumdrops
melting on birthday cake.

                              No one knows I've been left here.

Not much in the cupboards, less in the fridge.

Above my bed: a solitary figure
                              against a stone-cobbled fence.
You can't tell she's me, that the photographer lied,
told me its capture was an accident
though his horizon's straight as snow
sometimes blows.

That friend and others appear on my walls.
Benevolent ghosts; I will not let them leave.

I've brought also a cold to this place, and a zodiac
of bruises stains my left hip. Two nights ago
I stumbled drunk in my bathroom; downstairs,
forty guests drank cranberry punch and wine.

Just now a note has slipped from book to floor.
Handmade paper. Kind words reminding me
                              there's history to cling to.

        Five twenty-three; not even blue light
slants through my mini-blinds now.

Sometimes I can't believe

                              how quiet my world is.
I run to the west door;
an amber shawl has settled in the circuitry
of branches. Waning moon, snow a six-inch crust
on patio table, five empty chairs.

Faint tracks of dog
                    and deer. All around me
seniors live alone in large homes.
Beyond the filtering gauze of curtains
they creep through TV light.

                    Among this I skiff down *Calle* 55
with a dozen white mariposas
wrapped in newspaper. Morning,

                and each person I meet smiles back.

❧ More than twelve ways to look at the moon ❧

A crust of light enunciates an oversized coffee mug
and brass candlestick in a wax-splashed window.

Simple words spritz off the fourth page news, land silver
on the table and my arms. It has showered, the sidewalks

set for skating. My teenaged son phones from Vancouver
to play a little song on his harmonica,

a chick-a-dee in the lilac makes me weep. Winter
requires a hot bath, slow flame. Last night a wedding,

the bride in red velvet like a medieval queen.
The "Wedding March" tape went missing

and Jimi Hendrix filled in. Coming home I considered
the benediction of moon. It made me

say *arrhythmia, lavandula, palimpest, la luna.* Words
never tasted so fine inside this body's quiet spaces.

I find myself stopping as if my name's being called
in a stranger's baritone. Tonight another party; I'll laugh

too loudly. One could name daughters
after Mexican beach towns: Chuburná, Sisal, Celestún.

The fine art of escapes; how proficient I've become.
A few frozen dinners, city water, books and old sweaters
slung into a bag. (Also foreign films from the library;
I can only take solitude so far.) As long as I'm able
to keep myself in paper and tea, though there's also
wine and lorazepam, should it come to that again.

Highway splices stubble fields.
Between lambent scallops, one farm concludes
after the next. Saskatchewan is emptying.
Mid-afternoon light gilds the day and I forget myself,
alternately sing to five radio stations. I stop
with my camera; shoot a roadside cross, a staccato
of weathered bales. I've also forgotten

I love the adolescent curves of hills, mute combines,
swaths porcupining snow. In this hour
I am certain I will never leave what I've always known.
(Please don't ask about tomorrow.) In the yard, snow
skulks in the driveway and up the steps.
No one's been out except two rabbits, a deer.
Cold. Another benediction.

❧ Ghazal ❧

Pitahaya. One probing finger inside your colours,
I pull your white meat out.

Every morning past the painters on scaffolds;
we always say hello.

My map of the world slides off the wall
because it does not believe in me.

Hook, line and thinker. I am
sinking about you.

Why in all these languages
do you not love me yet?

SNOW SO BARELY THERE:
BANFF POEMS

⮜ **When there are no rooms left for us,**
   this is where we will meet ⮞

For three days we do nothing
but measure the timbre of voices
against forest sounds: colossal spruce falling.
Sometimes we walk.

I am tinder—

It's always like this when I see a woman
swinging a bag of oranges in the street, certain
she is loved. How easily she steps
among traffic, smiling to the bones of her feet.

these are the sticks of me

And often I forget where I am. I have not known light
as lava spilling down mountains
and aside from the magpies the birds here
are too brown and quiet.

in a dry season.

Because I love my name inside their mouths

I am becoming smoke.

Toques and jackets on the sixth floor terrace:

Helloooo down there!

Three writers clover beneath a moonless 1 a.m. sky;
a book by a Mexican poet
passes hand-to-hand, skin and words illumined
by a miniature flashlight—a AAA battery
keeping all this going.

        Ay, qué rico the lightning
and the Banff Springs Hotel: a spaceship
           landing or lifting off
across a river that changes colours
like a mood ring.

        Of course I am over the edge.

Low down,
in the surrounding forest, Bear 65
quarter-turns, eavesdrops
on the descending sap
of three voices—no, four—the wind
a marionette of old bones and teeth
crazy-dancing between jackpines.

Where are you, moon?

                    Tonight there will be dreams
of bumbleberries
and a long ago woman, corroding.

⁕ My brother receives us and we all come home ⁕

Cherries and peaches at a roadside stand,
a shortcut through dust.

                    My faith abided
in a varsity of horses. The Rockies—
a blue fingerpainting—pulled the horizon down.

Consonants of light and leaves, globes
of homemade wine.

            Only the cameras will believe
we gathered around your patio table
on a Canadian Sunday, laughing and eating steak
and new potatoes: *familia,* family
and the neighbours' watching dogs.

(Too bad they did not understand Spanish.)

Later we danced to "Cecilia" in your front room.

Thank you, brother,
for love measured in clean glasses.

A long time since I've written
but I want you to know, at 3 a.m.
                    Calgary was diamantine.

We finished your wine
on the highway.

And night held us safe in her glove.

❧ Everything is waiting for something ❧

The skin of oranges for the pinch of teeth,
my classical guitar for the alchemy of songs
you learned as a boy in music lessons. How we draw
things back to us. A posture, a glance. You know
what it's like.

Here we are skimming. Little gifts
of words, berries, a black-cased mirror.

A friend clutches a compliment across borders
and seasons, presents it like wildflowers
in a child's fist: *You are a boat
for use in shallow waters. You are very woman.*

On the other side of these walls
a *suspiro* of love on freshly-laundered sheets.
A curtain is opened or closed.

I scan Banff's mountains for animals, seek direction
from Kafkaesque clouds. Everything is high
this morning, like wine
made of grapes that ferment without added sugar.

Buttons of potentilla feast on yellow light.

How it is to be pilgrims together again. Echoes
of the old songs we sang.

↷ After canoeing we walked Banff Avenue
  as if drugged ↶

Soon enough I'll be a woman worrying about snow
on the highway but for now the mountains
are everywhere: *Está es la tierra del Dios*
y de María Santísima.

Yesterday in yellow canoes I wasn't certain
whether we were paddling upstream
or down; time and direction own no sense here.
River the colour of a tequila shooter
and ten people floated past

                        yelling camp songs.

God, what a movie.

Discoveries of bear prints,

                        darts in an underground pub.
All these impeccable days folding back
like sheets.

                    Do you need service?

the pretty Quebecois from Housekeeping asks.
Of course she means towels, soap, fresh glasses;
why should this make me weep?

I used to be able to do this.
Now there is too much light, time, friendship.

And happiness. I've forgotten
how to reconcile it, but when has it ever added up
    in this way?

My needs have grown small as berries
                                dripping off mountain ash
as my hands turn ever older
and more surprised
with what they are trusted to hold.

*⮑ Looking at your photograph I understand
where I must die ⮐*

This body so far from water seeks the sun's exhalation
on sea. Leaving will be like you have framed it

against the gallery wall: everyone has deserted
the café patio, day softens into an *a cappella* of shadows

between pillars and a corrugated roof. I could claim it
is the Mexican sky, *lanchas*, sand, *palapas*, sea. But mostly

this is about light and sin. You have launched me back
and it is futile to look too long

upon the held breath of an empty room
after its lovers have fled. Hopper knew this, also.

And yet we must look. Document sounds, peel paint,
sweep and sweep the sand we sallied in,

though the archaeology of wind erases everything
but tin and stones. No one fishing off the pier,

neither the flung white bandanas of gulls
fixed against October clouds. Believe this:

I am not lonely with the sun's choreography
of silver fish on broken cement,

it's only that the gathered dust of my whole life
could fit inside your room.

How often I change clothes
during inconsistent light ⌒

Keep on buying cakes and flowers; eventually the party
will find me.

———

Six at a table, artists and engineers
all alone together
in the corner coffee shop.

A Spaniard works in Sweden; the Irishman
wears hands like knives. A silver Madonna
on the Mexican's throat
resembles a communion wafer. We agree
not to become officers of the law
or teachers. Not even accountants.

The sculptor claims: *If you can draw, then surely
you can do anything.*

Diana absconds for a song on the piano.
For weeks this tune about tumbling leaves.

(The flipchart of memories smoke evokes.)

———

Earlier, a forest hike. My friend offered sage
and I thought *Prairie*, she, *Las Alpujarras*.
How nursery school
                        to make a chain of arms,
walk in the pistol-slap rain.

———

No day's a loss
when you make a smart man laugh.
Red wine, a picnic. The river—blue as vodka
meted against sky—trilled over knuckled rock.

———

                I have no reason
to identify with bats, or a cougar's altercations
in the razor-bodied trees,
but I do love a good game of shadows.

Sundown vibrates with mosquitos.
Topographical imperfections
in the plaster of skin.

———

Ever the faithful dog—my heart
at your heels. Ah, mountains, you don't change
anything.

Think of the furthest thing from your life.
A little further. Here I am.

**⮌ Sleep is a surface dive insomniacs
   easily ascend from
   (result of a small theft from José Teodoro) ⮍**

Sweet apples in pockets, some vague idea
about dawn and forest animals, a caul of mist lifting

off Vermillion Lakes and the discordant song
of nothing more than woodland ducks.

       To be with someone
who has only seen snow twice, then the finding
on Mount Norquay, snow so barely there you wonder
if you are willing it, like a phone call

or a story between strangers
you guess into shape, its returning weeks later
to wrong conclusions on your page.

Beneath you, the valley
with its palm upturned: *Take, take.*

And of course you do,
                 elk and snow-light

in the same window-balanced frame.

Antlers are a plot in a mystery
wandered out of control.

What you will sequester from this
is the drawbridge of stillness
before the buck swung his head and charged;

quieter inside that moment
than any place you've ever lived.

Poem that meanders toward Sandra Alland's
then perhaps the moon

A woman waits on a hotel bed
for a lover who will never arrive again.

                     In the slow mail of hours
she measures the weight of her hands,
eases them off her pelvic cradle, considers
the treason of roses
                     undressing themselves
in a simple jar
beside a half-open window.

How languidly she rises,
            locates keys, surrenders to a car
which leads down truth's only possible road:
    she is no longer young.

So often she's desired other countries
she has forgotten how to be home.

         In the diversion
of her family's kitchen, copper pots
beckon a last vestige of light. Tricks
in the garden's shadows: children
sailing kites toward a sky
         that will not receive them.

Arms splayed on the table,
                              palms relinquished
to futures left undone.

Night spreads like oil
toward the vellum of coastlines.

A little tea and toast if she can ever move again.
Then perhaps the moon.

❧ When you decide you must buy yourself flowers
(melancholy is a raincoat) ❧

Think of Lester Young playing sax to an empty room.
That first girl in grade four
to pierce her ears. Picnics in sweaters
and the small leaves that ride home on sleeves
and hair. A checkerboard of shadows.
An old or current lover invoking a Transylvanian accent:
Come, I want to embrace you.
Redheads wearing green. Men who love women
in glasses, and photographs
that caught you dancing. Three-year-old ballerinas.
Anyone who says they are *interested in your process.*
Words in the dictionary no one ever looks up.
The distance between swimming and drowning.

🦅 **It will all look like nothing**
when the photos come back
(an apology *a mis amigos mexicanos*
re: our prairie road trip) 🦅

The alphabet of my landscape begins here

—with field—
and ends with a sky forever exclaiming

the inconsequential: hawk's wing,
coyote's backward glance, surreal

crop dust ghosting above the highway. The usual nouns,
but there's something about the colours here;

I can see you are seeing it. Round bales
stuttering yellow across the plain, the grey bones

of outbuildings soft in their undoing, and I love how
you can't stop looking. A kind of worship

how barns wear their paint and horses don't care
that they are beautiful. How intimate this feels,

like drawing you inside my weather, those extremes
I speak and speak of, threaten each season

to divorce. Now you understand the tricks
light plays with fence posts: thin little sisters

grabbing your hands—*Don't go, or please*
take me with you. So much room it can be perilous

to speak, and look at the leaves, glittering like pendants
off the proffered wrists of trees. Not much to capture

on film, I know, but thanks for opening windows,
for anything you said,

and what your watching said for you.

☙ Poem ending in a phrase from Andrés Acosta (with a 50 metre fall) ☙

There are no small disasters.

Hiking around Lake Minnewanka
in a coincidence of five green shirts,
we stopped often for photos
                              and for no reason at all.

Vista from my studio—a panoramic
welcome: *Come to us.*
                    We are going to be best friends.

Mountain valley: a banquet etched out
and I pretend blindness. I would feel worse
but for the Japanese painter, here three weeks
and he's only stretched a canvas.

Bless you, Hiroshi.
Bless all the solitary lines adrift
like satellites that will never hit upon a home.
Bless the fuck-ups
on darkroom floors, the stains
we leave and leave
for nocturnal cleaners in comfortable shoes.

We are so many people here
                              missing our dogs
and all I can think of are September flowers,
the way my garden is her best self
when the vines begin to rust.

Don't trust the postcards.

While we pitched stones and pinecones
above the ravine, a child turned falling star.

O, mountains. This is the way
you erase us. We lose sight
of where we started from and memory
doesn't believe in us.

➷ Running in Banff with two weeks left (three things on the way) ➷

1.

I thought you were dead
but you were only dreaming on the asphalt path,
books and cigarettes stacked neatly as paradigms
beside the uncertain shape of your head. All of you
in green plastic, a kind of transient mummy
or skin tent; I wondered
how you breathed.

And why not the grass?
Why not weave a shelter on unwritten moss?

(What hardness we make ourselves endure.
I know little except hell exists
only of our own evocations.)

2.

When you're the type of person who says hello
to strangers you're never quite alone,
so what is the point of all this needing?

Near the cemetery, the dusty-leaf fragrance
of autumn marigolds: my impressionist garden.
Ah, home. Uncluttered love waiting
with faith and a torch of orange petals,

like I deserve anything
each time I decide to land.

Too easily days revolve around the math of tasks
as if flamenco didn't exist.

(Baby, let's work on that.)

3.

Always uphill.

This morning a triad of elk
disregarded me with such intent
I knew an end
or winter must be arriving soon.

Entire months when I should speak to no one
but my guitar. Burgundy thoughts
in my studio's aquarium of light.

Rocky Mountains scrawl
to the borders of vision and I am witness
to the single road out.

Holy TransCanada. How lifelong this
leaving will be.

⤳ A single grizzly is enough to sustain the legend
   (as Jorge Lara Rivera knows) ⤳

We expect elk at 7:45 a.m. as if they owe us
the spectacle of their dumb company
and poorly played trumpet, antlers
splintering trees like geriatric wrist bones.

And which of us watching fourteen mountain goats
zag up a cliff in their too-small shoes
does not dwell on the weakest
and secretly wish for a fall?

                    (Let's be honest
amigos, in our desire
for bears, the companionship
of subtitled movies on big screen TV.)

The road into Johnson Canyon
is strips of whittled wood. Scrawled
onto cardboard:

   Grizzly spotted here yesterday.

             So we hike. Snow sugars
the intestinal forest, dresses trees
for the whitest of weddings.

Photos before waterfalls,
inside pockets of rock. All that looking
over shoulders, bells looped to my purse, a clatter
like Christmas, shop doors
always opening.

I will not contribute to the lies of the world:
six weeks in Banff
and we didn't see a bear.

ᔟ Farewell ᔞ

Monday, our last, and I'm memorizing landscapes
as you congregate to eat. A little death is happening,
the mountains forgetting everything but blue.

Late for dinner, I will sit among mathematicians
and the bright light from Princeton will claim:
When you do good math, it's like poetry.

If I were the type who needs to talk
I'd tell him how silence wrapped us inside its smaze
whenever we landed near water.

A song for your pockets, a toast to the glory
of beaches and trees. This is what we have.

HANDS LIKE MY MOTHER'S: SASKATCHEWAN, AND ELSEWHERE

⮜ Sodium lights ⮞

Darling, all is not lost.

Just now I've recalled thunderstorms
in late afternoons, how we arrange chairs

in the verandah, watch the forecast
prove itself in the avenue's elms.

Around us the house settles
into premature darkness. Neighbours vapour

behind windows, and women in doorways
let their trapezius muscles relax.

We don't need to talk.
Drops big as tadpoles fall too heavily

between the one seam of eavestrough
you've never managed to mend; tiger lilies

hang their heads beneath the weight.
A puddle collects in the uneven sidewalk—

where I drew our names
before the concrete set.

Cars are washed clean and it grows darker
inside and out.

Sometimes lightning
so bright it trips off the streetlights.

❧ In May ❧

How well I am learning to kill

                              ants and weeds.

What a year has taught me.

The grass has paled into obscure shapes
like amoeba.

Squirrels make intermittent appearances
as if they're extras on a movie set.

The woods always moving. A sparrow kicks up leaves
like a digging dog.

At the school beyond is recess
or track and field.

                    —Yes, a starter gun
then cheers.

            Phone call from Mexico City:

sounds like shots
behind a voice I'd forgotten.

Gangs, he alleged, and I could only believe.

This is the thing:
                    what to distinguish as truth?

A wish for rain, fewer ants
writing scripts across the kitchen walls.

This place I have come to. Bursting.

❧ Nothing sounds as I remember it should ☙

The woodland's greening leaf by leaf, rabbits
and chipmunks not yet afraid. In the campground

the first guests return with trailers, satellite
around firepits in down jackets, looking sad. Already

the dock and diving board wait, buoys outline
a safe swimming place. A feeling like hope

this morning, perhaps a cloudburst
by late afternoon. Coffee with strangers

at the lakeside canteen
and I am thinking of next year, the life

I desire. Clever conversation
served with magazine meals; more Schubert,

museums, fewer lists. Who am I kidding?
In this house I am drawn to portals

as if someone will be arriving. Outside the black dog
rolls and splinters brittle grass. The sprinkler orbits

but my efforts may be too late. I plant ritual flowers
sewn from January seeds, a hard city winter

(but they're all hard winters now). In another room
the Lab\shepherd collapses; tall glasses thunder

in the cupboard. There is no one, and no one again.
The woods unrolling is all little explosions.

⬿ What I'm hearing right now ⬿

Windfalls, a small dog, snapping
caragana pods, swallows,
an occasional car muffler on Main.

My son on a payphone in Ontario:
    The thing is I'm having trouble
    with the money situation.

I hear myself say *I'll send three hundred.*

(When I see him again:
What are you doing with your life?)

Now the reprise: wind-rush—
all these weeks and it hasn't delivered
even a preamble of rain.

                    I am also listening

to the lake's invitation,
weeds' hide-and-seek in the grass, words
in books I've not read or written,
and, distantly, a murmur
I translate to mean:

What do I need to be loved for?

⤳ Old dog lies on the sun-bleached porch ⤳

Two ropes tether his red collar
so he won't wander into the copsewood
and claim a quiet place to die.

We explore the abandoned campground, snowdrifts
still lounging in shadows as if it's not
almost May.

         Robins have come
but I had forgotten pussy willows, rending
from husks sharp as feline claws.
I bite off twelve stubborn lengths, clutch them
in the manner of a settler bride.

My haste for this country; I've arrived
without towels and there is no milk.

I learn to sleep.
I listen to a zephyr fuss her skirts
at storm windows.

The knitting of hours in pollinated light, here
on my hands, like my mother's, which she maintains
have always been old.

Old dog, Alex, sees pixels of movement
through filmed-over eyes. Pussy willows
in a jam jar on the windowsill. An empty white bag:
limp ghost on the counter.

Tea grows cold, then colder in the pot.

∽ After ∾

The lawn is buzzed to a half-life, chickweeds
and dead impatiens drowned.
After the country auction—three hours
beneath the laureate sun
to bid on a badminton set (too short for anyone
in this long-boned home).

After the downy woodpecker
dulls his beak on the chimney's tin
rain cap, a flash flood in the trailer, and visits
from ten-year-old boys on bicycles (why do we
attract them?) there is you

in the throat of this house with Mexican walls, reading
Alfred Hitchcock's Mystery Magazine, me
on the deck with a Mardi Gras of birds,
a glass of beer the colour of sandalwood
I am quick to climb into.

Friends may come but we never expect them.
It's quiet and good how the sun rests softwater hands
on my shoulders. A lawnmower sings
its three note scale, and sometimes the wind
leaps between branches
in the poplar-silhouette, thinking itself animal.

❧ Driving at night away from the city, the sky ❧

is an infinite game of Lite-Brite. We forget
to be cautious of deer, the gravel road's ruffle

of deeper snow. Pots of verdigris light—
eyes trapped beneath pond ice—

define the runway near Cudworth and moon
hovers nowhere above.

No reason to speak. Village streets are empty,
snow like vanilla pudding

tempers front steps and rooftops.
Smoke rises from chimneys into polar bears.

This is what I believe in. You
pausing to gaze at the light show

before trenching a path to the door. Each time
the house smells like strangers

and we sleep as warm children
under tossed coats in a car. Between white fields,

below the black
punctured paper of night.

∽ Walking in woods
(with a brother-in-law fresh out of detox) ∽

Barley field ablaze with unblemished snow,
the brightness a slight ringing

pain beneath crusted lashes. At the edge
the winding lane and cacophonous birds. We are

swallowed by trees, the weight of ice
leaves casualties among poplars

I had not considered frail. Grosbeaks and small animals
left calligraphies before us. We punch

side-by-side trails; he is a silent smoking bear
in a long coat—where did it come from? His shoes

are wrong for this and he's brought no scarf,
as if he's forgotten the vendetta of wind. Christmas

has come and gone. On the lake, a single ice-
fishing shack, a frond of smoke. A grey owl

swoops through the cross-thatched ceiling like a bomber
from some other country's war. He mistakes

rabbit tracks for deer. I do not correct him.

≈ With frost laced on the windows,
   there is no seeing out ≈

Days when I follow the sun around the house,
        at each window a new sweater of light.

Outside the template for our friend Brad's painting:
        a wall of poplars, shadow, snow.

It is good what happens here. The work
we do, simple meals with mushrooms,
eggs and cheese.

I forget time and the map, my resolution
to visit a new country each year
and promises to faraway friends.

Languages.
        I forget them, too.

Jerry brings a recent woodcarving,
Anne shovels her drive.

Downstairs my husband paints self-portraits:
        a triptych in oil with palette knives.

In a few minutes I will hear him on the stairs
and we will laugh again
                        at his eyes.

It can't seem like much
but there is wood for the fire, cold beer
at the back of the fridge.

Sometimes a squirrel, always bluejays
and red-naped sapsuckers.

I tape new poems
to the drywall, sleep

      ten hours a night.

Then there is spring.

⊱ Alone ⊰

After you set dog-crumbles out for the deer, you build a fire in the woodstove. Suddenly: sweatlodge. The sweater goes, pants, socks. Inside the flames: a Pacific storm, the Red Rover-wind in the trees. That noxious smell is the Naugahyde stool melting. All you want to go with your beer are a few coals and to roast marshmallows on a long fork.

You've invited people over, hope they won't come. (You're always doing this. They rarely come.)

Earlier you tramped through the woods pretending you were lost. A snowy owl opened its wings like a flag unfolding and the horizon convulsed into fire.

Sometimes you realize how lucky you are. Mostly you want more of everything.

**⮑ Last night as though we turned a page
    today I love you more ⮐**

The trees before leaves are long-necked women
and I am startled to find them
when I feel I am alone.

Also pear-bodied birds interrupt my belief
that I could pass my life reading
in this yard-sale chair
beside the lace-covered glass.

The children are grown and we know
what that means.

So many maps spread across picnic tables, car hoods;
love is a new country now.

On the highway to Calgary I found my first
white hair, *My new pet,* I said, and expected to keep it,
though it was lost before Drumheller's badlands.

My home is not the city now; I am less
the more I am with people.

Except you. Please visit soon.

                    There will always be carnage
in the woods
I am waiting to show you.

Canticle

Holy, holy, holy the congregational crows'
raucous christening in the scarf of sky
between aspen treetops, arctic echoes
of ocean in low blue clouds. Holy the slow snow
released from dandelions, the head
of a mushroom: fleshy button
against the flesh of my palm. Holy
the desiccated fox, sparrow's severed wing, the woods
reclaiming what she lent. Holy the double thumbs
of a single deer print, the old road slick
after peregrine rain. For boulders,
their migrations complete, it's all held breath
and cinema now. What next to spring
from the teeming mulch? Holy white-petaled woodland
anemone, raspberry canes, ethereal wild asparagus
performing a gypsy dance. O, blackbirds.
Meadow is *sanctum sanctorum*. Startled mallard. Frog,
stone, nest a cradle for five speckled eggs. All
created round and easily missed. Holy are you.

⮑ Another lonely boy (for the collection) ⮐

                    In a canola field
watching a tempest spread itself
against sky. The crop—
like the hair on his shins—is new, a fuzz.

A beetle scribbles its manifesto
across his foot, then the opera
of rain and clouds.
(Across town the cows are not enjoying this.)

A radio report tangos with gusts
and the boy's mother
renders his name: *Dust-in.*

Soon he's knuckling my door
and wondering: *Will-you-be-my-friend?*

(I'm done with all that, my own kids grown
into adults I also never expected.)

I say *working, busy, maybe later tonight.*

He wants only to know how I stacked stones
for an Inukshuk, to help rake
the lawn's straw-brown blights.

No way not to disappoint him, he leaves me
in slim books and letters.

And the sky settles.
And a crow bobs in silhouette:
oil jack in the grass.

Dusk brings low-flying birds, a blur I recognize
                    as a loping deer.

I weed beds, clip spruce boughs, pincer
the beginnings of trees
from darker blades of grass.

          But don't you get lonely?

Surrounded by faerie woods, not sky between
but peepholes
into the clandestine lives of birds.

To have someone
not fourteen
say it like this:

          I want to know everything about you.

ᕫ Mothers' day (a soliloquy) ᕫ

A hat trick of rabbits with winter-white paws
figure-eight in sallow grass, not knowing
they've saved my day.

Clouds like tectonic plates
                                piece the eggshell-sky together.

All day by the window for the repertoire
of weather.

CBC radio is suffered in snatches:
Chechnya's president has been assassinated;
            more Mother's Day wishes
it fractures me to hear.

                        It will be dishwater
hauled to the southwest corner, where I've planted lilacs
for privacy.

Just beyond, the dog sniffed out a fox, quite dead
in its lovely and pestilent coat.

Yesterday I fingered a cervine jawbone, ants riddling
the wood of its three remaining teeth.

            When I say I can't do this anymore
I mean people, responsibility, books.

I abdicate the city.

As far as I flee, there's no leaving
the sky: a surprise M of geese
                              in the window frame.

☙ On passing a family fastening wreaths to a fence ☙

I am beginning to feel old
in my hands. Worn leather gloves,

they are finished with printing, guitars,
pleasuring men. The climate

keeps changing, my path
erased. To get where I am, an arithmetic

of hard steps and trains
of similar adjectives.

My face, too, is an easel of dirt roads,
small purse of my heart

can't foster another love or death
of any consequence.

I will own no more dogs
or cottages. All is becoming slack

except the time-teller sky.
Now is the opposite of a brewing storm.

Life's end: a handful of hail
flung back to the clouds, like party favours

when the last guest's gone home.

For Nadia (wearing the summer like a charm)

Remember the inukshuk with the erection?
There's an ice-cone on our favourite part today.

———

         We'd hiked to the end of the lake
the day we balanced those flagstones,

discovered ticks like minikin brooches
inside our pants, and surprised

one white coyote in the barley.

At midnight a garter snake
coiled round my ankle
while I was hosing the parched front lawn.

(I'd just bought this place, wasn't sure
if I'd gone crazier
or had finally cracked the code
                    to being saved.)

You were on the deck strumming folk songs.

———

Leaving bootprints in prairie sludge.
Arm-planing through cattails.
Slabs of shale
            in our backpacks.

God, I pity those women
without friends like you are to me,
men who can't recall what it is
to be Boy Scouts.

———

Soon May and the woods
will turn gazebo again
for the vowels that are small round birds.

Meditation on the first day of summer
   (for Betsy)

A woman in her garden shifts a cabbage-sized stone.

She furrows beneath roots, the viscidity
of earthworms. Stands back to see
what she has made.

      First day of summer and everything blowing:
elm seeds,
auburn wisps from the capsheaf
knot on her head.

She bends, stands, shifts again. An auger of sunlight
electrifies her white blouse.

You wonder what she is humming: *iris*, perhaps.
   Or *light*.

She removes cotton gloves, considers the sun
                  as if measuring its distance
from her spade.

Time's told in shadows.

You imagine her mother, the mother before her:
Same sun. Same faith in seedlings?

A city kindles itself around a garden's potential
and here it begins.

Morning, on Seventh Avenue. A gabled house
framing a solitary woman—good, pacific,

not knowing she is watched.

⮫ Cypress Hills ⮪

When you camp with an 18-year-old son
it's a double tent deal.

                                      Departing,
both of us this late August.

We share one moon
in a barren campground, sledge stakes
through snow-floured dirt.

Oh, the work of it.

Harvesting logs from other sites, hanging a windbreak
with the extra orange tarp.

(Later we two-spoon a can
of beef stew.)

                            Fire keeps us close.

Lodgepole pines
                    like totems
support the canvas
of a renascent night.

I'm off for a month of writing in Mexico,
                  you start Katimavik in Vancouver.

Into the deep-sea hours
            with wool toques, winter coats. We bare
the templates of opposing philosophies
as if unbound by blood.

                        A pox of sunflower seeds
rings the firepit. End of a story
    in the ash-fine ink.

Morning after a non-sleep, we wander
            through deadfall
into a clearing glossed with light,
spot a bull moose
and track him for hours—an animal like a map

            naming who we are.

☞ **Snow day**
     (for Mark) ☞

—Do you remember it?

Like waking inside an angel food cake: the yard,
village, fields beyond, snow heaped
well past our thighs.

Good thing we had the boots and hearts
for it.

God, what a march. What mastodons
we were, to attempt it.

              Sometimes I fell
and crawled through it. A swimming
kind of snow; I ate it like bread
off red mittens.

Everything polished
to a Sunday-morning shine.

              On the lake
a few people fishing through halos of ice.

You want to know what a poet does.

We steal
the best parts:

not the crack and instant water
that flooded your boots, or the wolverine
panic in your eyes.

But after,
how we glowed
at the table around a casserole.

In the next room our socks—limp puppets drying–
beside a fire that sounded like rain.

**I want to get to know you for a very long time
(a poem in two seasons)
(for Taylor)**

1.

All day the sun's game—I step onto the deck,
she hides behind clouds; I go in, she bounces back,
laughing her head off.

Gulls ask: are you for *ree ree real?*

On the eve of your 18th birthday we sat on my bed,
ringed in a moat of poetry.

You wore unmatched socks, forgot again
to comb your hair. We read to each other
for the good blood of words,
but I am nothing like you.

It rains for two weeks. Each Lilliputian lilac petal
a dish for a single regret. Inventory: my life
adding up to not enough.

2.

Winter now; the weather's good for excuses
and reading 19th century British novels
in my bedroom's torso of light. Mostly this is apology
for attempts at shedding the skins of my fears—
night, gang violence, strangers—onto you.

Well, it hasn't worked, and soon another birthday.
You'll want little again—something by Kafka,
knitting needles.

Another day tips a shoulder toward evening.
You slip beneath my covers in jeans. Pale as paper
but you won't eat meat.

None of us eats together anymore,
each of four leaving crumbs and lettuce leaves
on the counter for the next.

3.

These are the last rooms we lived in.

EUROPA, EUROPA

London (the day you despised me)

Because I insisted we hike from Victoria Station to the Paddington hostel.

At first it was a light shower and we were only mildly lost in Chelsea. I sang Joni Mitchell, noted the *Benny Hill Lived Here* sign. (You were not amused).

Because we bought orange juice we did not want from a honey-eyed boy whose directions we could not use.

Because a cathedral of rain fell.

Inside my backpack, re-laundered words wept off pages, airline tickets buckled like knees.

We dragged sopping bags through the meadow Hyde Park was becoming, took refuge beneath an oak's umbrage.

Clothes transparent, flurries in our eyes. I took your photo. Because.

◈ Hawthornden Castle ◈

How centuries away I am, the stone wall
so many broken teeth and feathered ivy.

No one comes. Midlothian wind and River Esk, the same
melancholic hymn played across the bones

of yellowed keys. Cup of tea on the sill,
dead moths and ashes in the hearth.

Distant daughter and son; imperceptible brown trout
in ferruginous water. It is all

inventions. Beyond the green gate
the mud of cars and queues, electricity bills.

West is Glasgow and little boys
named Jimmy. Here only an apron of sunlight

on my lap, weight of a child, wee
and almost sleeping.

⤳ Tyne Esk Trail ⤝

Grid on the morning, a subterfuge
of bushes. I run eclipsed from the convoy
blitzing toward Edinburgh, stop only
for the minor notes of thorns.

Three times I spy the not-colour, alabaster,
and hallowed sun: muted poppy
shivering beneath grey cashmere. Rabbits
and blackberries live here;
there have been horses. What legends
from centuries-old dwellings
crowning aureate fields
and trestling a sky
                    that could go either way.

Only one other on the dew-slapped trail; boy
or almost-man, hands shrouded
in pockets, his new running shoes
     two flares
loud as words in a low-ceilinged room.

Woods and tombstones rise from nothing.
A flotilla of impatiens and conch shells
link the dead
to memories they were meant to have.

Morning glories
whiter than the buds stars begin from
and magpie, bird of opposites,
                              screams decrees.

I double back, amphibian-skinned,
to the overgrown secret
                  garden on the hill, steal
three gold-flecked plums: velveteen
on the wafer of my tongue.

‚ Pastoral ‚

1.

Bandage of light in woods so otherwise dark, owls
believe it is night. A woman, especially,
could die here and remain
unnoticed, River Esk masking
the avian noises born deep
inside her cage. Die
or begin again. Change her name,
passport. Scrabble up the fern-mottled bank
into the drone of different traffic.

Water eddies over a char-black rock
or turtle's back. Dunnocks lollop
in the prickling hedge. Such camaraderie. I need
September, the cracks and pops of seeds,
insolent mushrooms. To thrash
through nettles, tuft and ribbon grass
with a stick like a twelve-year-old boy.

2.

No one's minding the greenhouse
and the grapes have gone wonderfully mad.
Earlier the cook caught me snitching.
I thought she was a portrait, *Country Girl
Filling Basket With Cooking Apples.*

Genius at fear, what to do
with this absence?

Yellow-red leaves, flat boats
on the cola-coloured water. Stare long enough
and I'll see goldfish, parlors, bus stops, amethysts,
a woman gripping a skeleton key
between beautiful ravaged teeth.

To read a book slowly

"That's what art is for: to remind us that we have not seen what we remember having seen."
                              —Lesley Adrienne Miller

Three days, longer if I desire, to revel
in this stumbled-upon book

of poems. A few lines and I'm drawn
to the equally exquisite sky, so opaque

I could believe I am looking at snow.
This is Hawthornden. Gourmet meal

across a month-long table, window benches
collecting rations of light. This book

by an American poet
who has also known these castellated walls

and four o'clock tea. I consume
her words deliberately, luxuriant foreplay

through a caravan of afternoons. Words
at the desk and in the high bed. Sometimes rain

light as breath and dust-
coloured against moss-softened cottonwoods.

I am tethered.
I am the rotund birds' trapeze

between oak trees, journey on the single bike,
saddle tipping me forward

through all the sad, pretty towns.
A book of poems on a chair

in the light where I left it.
Sounds only woodland animals hear.

⤚ Away ⤛

I sometimes think of the mail collecting,
a snowy pile pitching over itself
on my desk where I've instructed the children
to leave it. Mysterious envelopes
sans return addresses, little manila cushions
they will shake at their ears
like the one Christmas gift they can't manufacture
a name for. This is the third autumn
I've been gone. My garden won't know me
when I return, husband and children will entertain
a formal berth in the halls between us, as if
facing a large unfamiliar dog. I did not expect
to become a woman of so many maps.
Or scars. Often things have gone wrong
and wild. When away
I am telekinetic, stunt my body back
like a child setting dolls in a playhouse. There I am
at my dressing table. There light
weaving through fingers at the sink; dishes
done, I am only standing, mesmerized by some memory
I have not yet earned. Mail on my desk, shoes
remembering foot bones. Stairs waiting
for the weight of my mechanics. Last night, returning
from the pub, I stopped beneath the candelabra
elms in the black-winged lane, requested the others
cut their flashlights. Tawny owls
kept busy rifting branches, a sound

like all the doors in the world
being opened at once. It smelled
like a deep green bowl on a table
in a country I have never pronounced. I am always
never quite anywhere.

✎ Hawthornden Castle 2 ✎

We'll name what we're searching for
and it will be lies.

Pictish drawings or Wallace's cave, nouns
plucked like green pears.

I'll be the quiet one, then,

having not read your libraries
or politics.

I have spell-fallen
for the stag-and-doe pattern
interplayed on curtains and quilt.

Perhaps I should have lived another life
in darker clothes. Sleep
keeps pulling at the hooks of me,
making me rags.

I have no currency

for wine, no desire
for phantoms. (Who is this Evelyn
who lends me her bed?)

When you live in a castle you are forever
canting out.

Night is a 17th century fortress. A gale
swells through the hearth's black lung. What if

all I accomplished was a study
of each Fellow's hands?

Who would expect it?
Who expects wild crocus in September?

Four-leaf clover
pinned to my heart. Nothing hurts
me here.

⮞ Castle Walk, by night ⮜

One woman hopes to spot the autumn red fox,
one woman hopes not to twist an ankle.

One wears green wellingtons and recalls
forty thousand snow geese
concurrently erupting
off a spring-fed lake on the prairie.

Deafening, turbo-charged,
                              a conflagration of wings
against a denim-blue mantel.

(Finest moment in the previous year.)

Night arranges its black cotton. Wood-pigeons
bloat alders, tambour moon tinsels light.

The woman in wellingtons wonders
how to subsist
in a world trellised with people
                              and speech.

The path expires and each is aware
in her closet of skin
that winter is now upon them.

There's been one trivial stumble,
no fox in red boots.

Two women return
to the fireside elocution.

Below and behind, a single trout whoops.

≈ Imbroglio ≈

The lane's turned leafy puzzle.

I've been wanting this
                    fall upon us—
semester to bury summer's short sleeves
and nutshell the heart.

I saw the russet fox
before he spied me. Above us clouds
zippered the sky
    like a sleeping bag.

I am reading love poems from one man
to another. There was a time—

but now I prefer lanterns,
the way they metamorphose
                    even the simplest garden.

In my garden I've strung white lights
through Virginia creeper
                    which knits itself
into lilac. Everything ventricaled
to something else; I'm no longer sure
which belonged first.

And where do seasons begin?

September,
                    and anachronistic crocus
opens its six-fingered hand
to receive a surprise.

                         Already snow
is making wool
of eyelashes
on my side of the Atlantic; we latch on
          to what will receive us.

But autumn inspires to come clean, unknotted.

To snap words down
for what they are:
today I saw the red fox before he saw me.
He was very red.

⁓ Lady Walk ⁓

I may never again feel this loved
by trees. No margin for mistakes
on this labyrinthine path, narrow as victories
sometimes are and atmospheres
above the lisping stream. Stone-slippered,
grass-thrashed, leech-slick; Lady Walk
you're ironically named. And I'm so dizzy
today, my blood determined to run thin
as skim milk. I'm feeling all treetops,
little bird, green. I've found Wallace's cave
and planted words like seeds
inside it: *Pinus sylvestrus,*
Sambucus nigra, Taxus baccata.
Each day I do something that makes me wonder
why I don't do it every day. Here I am,
my life half lived, and still this need
to climb trees. *Betula pendula, Quercus robur.*

To lean over the gorge is to eavesdrop
on a world upside down, the way as children
we'd tramp through our rooms
with mirrors at our waists, so it appeared
we were walking on ceilings. And maybe we were.
Maybe all I require is a thicket
of amber light deep inside forest
so I can pull off a fairy tale
century of sleep.

What greed. And guilt, too, because *hard*
is the adjective I too often pin
to the brown solid nut
that's my life. Even now I veer off
what there is of a path, grasp
the extended hands of ferns
to follow the faint hope
of deer trails. Perhaps I've scrambled
my fundamentals: not stopped enough, not stared
at filaments and white flies floating
or recognized oak leaves
for the paws they certainly are.
O, moss, forgive me. Sycamore, reduce me.
Giant fir, be my reticent friend.

Retreat
(for E. H.)

When a misses hangs black cardigans
beneath an awning of rain, I wonder
where she travels.

Similarly, the gardener, fingers plugged into loam
when moon's already a monocle.

At the end of this hallway, a Londoner
gathers facts around him
                            like candies or coppers
pitched from a float in a smalltown parade.

Writers are masochists.

We communicate through doors
left open an inch
            or no fraction at all, none knowing
where the others' plots lead.

End of the hall: you.

        Minutes long-needle themselves into days
and I have only a scone of knowledge
about the novelist you are—
            or whom you wish in the well
you could be—

                        although at night
you sound so near
I feel your heart

                    thinking.

✐ Roses are bleating their fool heads off again ✐

Their coral beauty heightened against this palette
of rain and cement.

My umbrella flips out—comic and rude—
like flashing my panties
at Bonnyrigg's leashless dogs and fat babies,
women with cigarettes scissored
between the ochred Vs of their fingers.

My mission: to locate a one-hour photo shop
though I expect nothing of this film—
my camera tumbled off a cliff
and sunk into mud-water
before I could shape an *Oh*.

Rain writes her monologue in the almanac
and though I adore walking
and poems that hinge on the word *Sometimes*,
I hail a bus, ask the driver to drop me
at the castle's green gates.

Tourist spot, is it? \ No, it's for writers. \ Ah, horse *riders.*

I've been called worse. Why explain
that strands of his hair will nest in a poem
and stanzas will come of a frenetic robin
trapped in a dining room
set with silver?

It's all roses and blowsy here.
Rough boys kicking balls
where games are not to be played.

⤚ Nearly happy ⤙

The trees are roaming where the clouds left off,
like photographers whose subject is the dark.

I'm dressed in the feeling of having broken
something priceless—an opaque French pitcher—

and not knowing whether to confess. Yesterday
was pale horses wearing blinders

and tunnels like long black throats.
The sign said *Keep Going,* so I followed

an ice cream truck's incubus song; the driver
bore misdemeanours in his eyes. All the men

in that town wore their skulls like monks
and walked with one shoulder to the wind. But

the women were nearly happy and so close
to the hills they could mail their voices

and trust they'd return—plastic bags
or red scarves. Wind toys. Soon clouds

were roaming where the trees left off.
I gathered my feet and bone china

spirit. (Repaired, if only temporarily.)
We shatter what's closest by wanting too much.

The heart's grope for glass on the mantel.

⮽ Self-portrait ⮼

The art of being where you do not belong
is tripped into, not learned.

       Like here. Rooms pulsing orange
with intellect and diatribe. I don't want any

politics. I only want to strangle
the lights and play ghost games.

Castle stairs are keyboards; the music
is wrenching. There's a dungeon, emergency

candles. Woods teeming with spooks.
Too much skeleton in me, I can't shake

these rock and roll bones, can't be a proper misses
who snaps just one tooth
of chocolate from the communal bar.

(And anyway, it tastes like blood.)

Everything I know could be poured
into a tulip.

Am I selfish to love best the hours alone?

I don't mean to steal
a page from Plath's text, but I am
a walking cicatrix.

Then I see a man flying
the world's smallest kite
and my spirit
rambles where the clouds left off.

⮜ Evelyn room ⮞

You've held me well through this month
of nights.

Framed in twelve-panes is everything
that interests me:

the way light manicures trees
and flies carry on like busy executives, cellphones
melting into thoraxes.

              Just one red-leafed tree exclaiming
among the demure green.

I've left a diaspora of crumbs for visiting mice
and a stain on the writing desk

          where I spilled Diet Coke,

its paramecium shape
something for future poets to ponder.

Listen, I am forty-one years old and afraid
to be naked.

Outside this room, my new skin
and story. Inside, false starts
balled into the wastepaper basket.

My prints will be wiped clean of this
by some housekeeping Mary or Margaret,
but Evelyn, here's a penny
to hide in the hearth. A single copper, proof

I was here.

ᕲ Suddenly ᕲ

Everyone terrifies me.

I retreat to the tangled trees; I understand
their lessons in deconstruction, need no other
skin for company.

In the Central Highlands, salmon flew
up the River Braan's falls.

Have you seen this?

It's sacred, violent, not to be believed.
Most belly-slammed rock
and knocked back into the roiling pool.

It's all in the attempt.

October.

Bracken is brassy and the heather's gone grey.

I say *suddenly*, but the spirit possesses no yardstick,
no rain gauge.

Back in Canada,
I don't know what kind of woman I'll be
without woods
and seventy pounds of dog.

I have been weeks in countries
where rain falls precipitously.

This is the counting down,
the last of sink-washed socks and panties
drying from hangers.

Between pages,
I press beech, oak, chestnut leaves.

                    Chapters I could not write.

Breakfast in the dark, for I am early
with my bowl of granola; unexplored woods

beckon with dew-fragrance. And yes
it is good to caress gnarled trees, finger shoots

of ivy as a blind woman hungry
for the details of a face. In the orchard

green apples spill onto grass and are left
like abandoned marbles. A few carmine globes

are stigmata in undressing trees. Summer's spent
all her candy money. Two deer investigate

my interest in the tarped pool, plastered
with oak and maple leaves. Dublin is a touchstone

in the near north. Cows pay no heed
as I trek along their fence in a red jacket,

matadorian without intent. The blue Madonna
in her grotto reminds me I am loved.

Brother Columba pours milk from a pot
for the eighteen outdoors cats. Within such activity,

his voice is susurrant: what gospel he shares
is fruit I cannot taste.

⁓ Dublin ⁓

"Someone ought to turn the telly on: perhaps we will hear definitely that we have drowned."

—Pádraig J. Daly

Across tree-outlined fields, beyond grazing cattle
in tri-colour combos, the melodrama that is Dublin
wrestles into a new evening of headlines
for tomorrow's *Irish Times*.

                I am ready in my window seat.

Down there: *Beaten to a pulp*
for a can of beer, but up here it's soundless. Embers
of light scrawl an ancient code and blush
the undersides of clouds.

On the right, the lighthouse
                      guiding ships into Dublin Bay.

Above it all, airplanes like midges float
onto runways. Fireworks—white and green—
plume from city centre.

A ringside seat
over Dublin's skyline; I should not want
for anything after this, but I will, too soon,
human that I am
                  and ever insatiable.

I seem to fit on these sidelines.

Dinner with the Augustinians:
Jude, John, and Kiernan, the handsome,
cycling priest.

                Men who understand the quiescence

of morning strolls through sodden woods
and past bemused cows. Late rhododendrons
like hearts that won't let go.

Father Pádraig gives me two of his books
and I send a clutch of fresh poems
with typos inked over.

Hoodlums smash Father Jude's windshield.
So hard to get out here
            and nothing in it for them.

Just now: fleeting light.
        Pipe bomb
or epiphany.

                  I am wrapped in wonder.

❧ Temporal ❧

I fall asleep sitting because there is sunlight
to feed me,
a wool blanket for my legs.

Clouds crush in
like a congregation of rhinos
on pilgrimage from the west.

The light, like my days left in Ireland, is numbered.

I do little more than breathe on glass. Why
isn't this easy?

At lunch Father Jude informs me
about what to expect at Mass. *No one will notice,*
he says, *if you sleep.*

How did he know
that what I most desire is sleep?

And books.

I read everything: Irish essays,
an English murder mystery, illustrations
from the *Book of Kells.*

What I would sacrifice
for my own shelves, the pages I haven't yet read.

I want to be home now. My daughter writes:
je trouve votre absence dure.

Always this measuring
of what could still go wrong:
                                          bombs, plane crashes.

Last night a gale to fracture the foundation;
this morning the same tease of light
seduced me out to the chestnut,

the maples' knurled limbs.

Too soon rain's Draculean cape again.

In Canada, at least there's hail
          when rain makes this much of an effort.

⮂ Revelations ⮀

Maple leaves—curled, yellow, spinning—
are sometimes butterflies. Sunlight

splashed across a white paper
in a country where light's thimbled out

is ablution. The Augustinians in grey knitted jumpers
could be anyone's grandfathers.

Best is Brother Columba of the mewling cats.
Best is the news that this battered heart

can still give a little kick
over mouse-nibbled mushrooms. I pocket leaves

I don't have names for, speak to heifers
as I pass. Each time a new blue mountain

of clouds gives way,
I want to throw a welcome party

for the sun. It's like seeing a friend
you said goodbye to

and never expected to see again, then there he is
at the roadside as your bus pulls away.

The volcanic sun. A red-orange curtain
winged before my eyes.

ᔰ Yellow ᔰ

There must be something to learn here
but I'm little wiser except to name a chestnut tree.

Days there's no poetry left in me, as if rain's
washed me clean of it.

I want to be in my house
with its familiar smells and messes; I fill the abyss
of these long days with pots of tea and sleep.

> One day we drive.

Almost too late to begin, fog
wraps us in dry ice and light descends
as we climb
toward zero vegetation.

Clouds are ushered across the Wicklow Mountains
like ruffians from a bar.

(And I believed Saskatchewan headmaster of wind).

   If I could see I'd know this
                        to be beautiful,

but we're a nun-to-be and a writer
in a compact car
on a cliff-edged road;

approaching headlights
blind at each curve.

Even without rain,
                    a *petit point* of moisture
dapples my second floor window.

I fist-rub and stare at Our Lady
across lichen-crusted shingles.

Sometimes a cat animates the distance between us,
sometimes a movement I attribute to air.

They tell me it's the season.

I perch on the ledge with dead flies
because my best meal is light.
Here butter,
              a saffron bath towel.

I imagine luminescence
like a child draws a spiked yellow triangle
in the top corner of a page.

          Now rain in all its incarnations
blurs the shape of Our Lady.

I am weary, hovering;

          hungry for the colour of home.

NOTES

The quote from Lesley Adrienne Miller is from her poem "The Anarchist," in *Eat Quite Everything You See* (Graywolf Press, 2002).

Pádraig J. Daly's line appears in his poem "Someone should," in *Nowhere But in Praise* (Profile Press, 1978).

ACKNOWLEDGMENTS

I am grateful to the organizers of and my fellow participants in the Canada-Mexico Writing\Photography Exchange, in which ten Canadian artists collaborated with ten Mexican artists in Mérida (2002) and at the Banff Centre (2003). Fondest thanks to my Can-Mex familia: Maleea Acker, Andrés Acosta, Gerardo Montiel Klint, and Juan José Rodríguez—picture-perfect adventures and eternal friendships. To my family-family, who have supported me in Saskatchewan, away, and back again (especially you, Troy), and to my eclectic cast of friends: you are where home is.

Several of these poems were written at the Hawthornden Castle International Retreat for Writers (Scotland), and I am ever so thankful for receiving a Fellowship to be there in 2004. To the Augustinians at Orlagh Retreat Centre, in Dublin—and to Marian, the prospective nun who took me out to the pubs for Guinness(es)—thank you for welcoming me into your fold. Most of the rural poems were penned in Middle Lake, Saskatchewan—a woodsy, lakeside village I used to visit. In 2007 I moved there.

Thank you to The Canada Council for the Arts for a grant which provided me with the time and means to work on this manuscript, and for grants that facilitated travel to the international retreats. This book could not have been completed (at least not in *this* decade) without that generous financial assistance.

Some poems in this manuscript previously appeared in journals. I thank the editors of *Event, Grain, Navegaciones Zur* (Mexico), and *Other Voices. Muchas gracias* to Jorge Lara for including my work in his anthology, *Quatro Postigos* (Instituto de Cultural de Yucatán, Mexico, 2007), and to Don Gill for using my poems "Sisal" and "Poem ending in a phrase from Andrés Acosta (with a 50 metre fall)" in his short video, "Ten Texts and Two Melodramas". "Sodium lights" appeared in *String to Bow*, a Leaf Press chapbook.

A selection of the Banff Poems was shortlisted for the CBC Radio Literary Awards, and a suite of the Scotland and Ireland pieces was broadcast on CBC Radio Saskatchewan (cheers, Kelley Jo). "Walking in woods (with a brother-in-law fresh out of detox)" earned Second Place in the Poetry Category of the 2005 Saskatchewan Writers Guild Literary Awards.

And finally, to Richard\Ricardo, the Chicago blues musician well-met in the Santa Maria hotel in Melaque, Mexico, in 2001: thanks, man, for putting the title in mind.

Cover art: Detail of a relief by 18th century sculptor Ignacio Vergara on the façade of the Museo Nacional de Cerámica González Martí (Palacio Del Marqués De Dos Aguas) in Valencia, Spain.

Shelley A. Leedahl is the author of seven previous books. She has been awarded the John V. Hicks Manuscript Award, a Short Grain Award, *Foreword Magazine*'s "Book of the Year" (Children's Literature, United States), and more than a dozen Saskatchewan Writers Guild awards in various genres, including literary non-fiction. Two of her titles have been shortlisted for "Book of the Year" (Saskatchewan Book Awards).

Leedahl has been the recipient of the Wallace Stegner Grant for the Arts (Eastend, SK) and received fellowships from the Hambidge Center for Creative Arts and Sciences in Georgia (US) and the Hawthornden Castle International Retreat for Writers (Scotland). As well, she was one of five Canadian writers selected for the Canada-Mexico Writing/Photography Exchange in Mérida (Mexico) and Banff. Her work frequently appears in literary journals and anthologies across North America and on CBC radio. She lives in the village of Middle Lake, Saskatchewan, and regularly travels to conduct author visits and creative writing workshops.

Praise for Leedahl's previous work:

Orchestra of the Lost Steps

"Leedahl turns these ordinary people into extraordinarily colourful characters. She can snap a portrait of abject despair, of sexual frustration, or of lingering regret, and the reader watches the Polaroid of that life reveal itself in the bright light of her prose. Her roots as a poet are evident in this collection . . . she combines poetry's economy of language with its connotative powers . . . "

—*Books in Canada*

Talking Down The Northern Lights

"Shelley Leedahl's poetry astonishes ... she swings from the cosmic to the earthbound with ease. Writing in a confidential, conversational tone, she holistically juxtaposes uncanny perceptions, humourous asides and delicious innuendo. In the lingering afterimage, her consummate skill and courageous questing are magnified."

—*Prairie Fire Review of Books*

"Leedahl continues to break the stereotype of the traditional female poet."

—*Winnipeg Free Press*

Tell Me Everything

"[Leedahl] combines the love for language that motivates most poets with the spare writing style she's honed as a short-fiction specialist ... the way this novel reaches its conclusion is a masterful bit of plotting that needs to be savoured on the page."

—*Saskatoon StarPhoenix*

The Bone Talker

". . . a wonderfully quirky story . . . "

—Globe and Mail

" . . . award-winning Saskatchewan poet and novelist Shelley Leedahl has written a touching story . . . a beautiful fusion of text and illustration."

—Quill and Quire

A Few Words For January

"Leedahl's book may be the first I've read over the past year which I would confidently recommend for even the most avid poetry hater . . . "

—Edmonton Journal

Photo credit: Taylor Rae Leedahl

Shelley A. Leedahl is the author of seven previous books. She has been awarded the John V. Hicks Manuscript Award, a Short Grain Award, *Foreword Magazine*'s "Book of the Year" (Children's Literature, United States), and more than a dozen Saskatchewan Writers Guild awards in various genres, including literary non-fiction. Two of her titles have been shortlisted for "Book of the Year" (Saskatchewan Book Awards).

Leedahl has been the recipient of the Wallace Stegner Grant for the Arts (Eastend, SK) and received fellowships from the Hambidge Center for Creative Arts and Sciences in Georgia (US) and the Hawthornden Castle International Retreat for Writers (Scotland). As well, she was one of five Canadian writers selected for the Canada-Mexico Writing/Photography Exchange in Mérida (Mexico) and Banff. Her work frequently appears in literary journals and anthologies across North America and on CBC radio. She lives in the village of Middle Lake, Saskatchewan, and regularly travels to conduct author visits and creative writing workshops.

RECENT OOLICHAN POETRY

Shirin and Salt Man • Nilofar Shidmehr

"The poetry comes with the complexity of a
novel and the simplicity of a song, plus its own
powers of illustration in a language that is both
figurative and wisely, brutally realistic. This is a
modern Iranian epic, a cautionary tale, written
in Canada by a young poet whose voice deserves
to be heard from Vancouver to Tehran."

—George McWhirter

Along a Snake Fence Riding • W. H. New

"New's images and his brilliant language imbue
his poems with the ability to temporarily halt the
rushed city dweller into quiet reflection . . . At
the end of the journey there is a dazzling array
of colour and a sense of seeing nature in all her
majesty for the first time."

—Irene D'Souza

The Incorrection • George McWhirter

"To sit with George . . . takes one into an ancient world of oral recounting, as the tales of Irish life pour out in an Ulster English as soft as rainwater, the voice rising and falling, sometimes low as a whisper."

—George Woodcock